STOKE-ON-TRENT

Edited by Lucy Jeacock

First published in Great Britain in 2002 by
YOUNG WRITERS
Remus House,
Coltsfoot Drive,
Peterborough, PE2 9JX
Telephone (01733) 890066

HB ISBN 0 75433 880 0
SB ISBN 0 75433 881 9

FOREWORD

This year, the Young Writers' Hidden Treasures competition proudly presents a showcase of the best poetic talent from over 72,000 up-and-coming writers nationwide.

Young Writers was established in 1991 and we are still successful, even in today's technologically-led world, in promoting and encouraging the reading and writing of poetry.

The thought, effort, imagination and hard work put into each poem impressed us all, and once again, the task of selecting poems was a difficult one, but nevertheless, an enjoyable experience.

We hope you are as pleased as we are with the final selection and that you and your family continue to be entertained with *Hidden Treasures Stoke-On-Trent* for many years to come.

CONTENTS

Greenways Primary School

Jessica Wright	32
Daniel Brookes	33
Yasmin Bailey	34
Laura Mountford	35
Callum O'Donnell	36
Emily Cartlidge	37
Reece Watts	38
Bryony Tideswell	39
Alex Holt	40
Benjamin Sharps	41
Zach Hind	42
Larissa Panepinto	43
Frederick Jones	44
Louise Wiggins	45
Laura Hurst	46
Alice Gething	47
Philippa Bourne	48
Samuel Taylor	49
Michelle Beech	50
Jamie Cartlidge	51
Alex Burns	52
Lucy Moston	53
Jack Gibson	54

Hanley St Lukes CE Aided Primary School

Jemma Ann Roberts	55
Stephanie Crowley	56
Jack Parsons	57
Halil Edward Eren	58
William Wainwright	59
Rosie Mayer	60
Ryan Lawrence	61
Ryan Malbon	62
Amy Watts	63
Jodie Miller	64
Jade Moore	65

The Poems

THINKING ABOUT FOOD

I hate sandwiches,
I loathe all fillings stuck inside them,
Ham, spam, cheese and paste,
Jam, sauce and chocolate spread.

I love my mum's Chinese chicken,
Brown spicy sauce and roast potatoes,
Sizzling chips.

Wayne Copestake (11)
Aynsley School

SCARY MOVIES

Scary movies make me shiver,
Palms all sweaty, pumping heart.
Monsters, goblins, giant chickens,
Knives and scissors, guns and darts.

Gooey, scarlet, dripping blood,
Creepy zombies, howling ghosts.
Rotting mummies falling to bits,
Vampires skewered with wooden posts.

Steven Hollins (13)
Aynsley School

MULTICOLOURED DOGS

Brown, black,
Black and white,
Bright as day,
Dark as night.

Spotty Dalmatians,
Curly poodles,
Round, brown sausage dog,
Hey! There are oodles.

Cuddly, funny, warm and soft,
Floppy ears and wagging tails,
Shiny coat, licking tongues,
Always love that never fails.

Samantha Pimlott (11)
Aynsley School

BEAUTY

I have a pony who is black,
she loves it when I sit on her back.
When I had her she was virtually wild,
but with time and patience,
she is calm and mild.

I love riding Beauty
because she is such a little cutey.
She is my best friend
and I'll love her right till the end.

When Beauty is turned out,
it's lovely to see her gallop about.
Sometimes she rolls in the mud,
now I don't think that's very good.

But Beauty's my little pony
and she'll never be lonely,
cos I love her and she loves me
and that's why she's part of my family.

Demi Fox (10)
Ball Green Primary School

PARADISE

I am on a beach in paradise,
I know it will not last.
Just putting things behind me,
All about the past.
I sip a drink, eating mangoes,
Listening to the banjos,
All about the day!

Lying down and listening
To the sea,
Upon which a little boat
Is waiting for me.
I am a little bird,
All alone but free.

Samantha Savage (10)
Ball Green Primary School

EXCITEMENT

The ride was like a huge monster,
Reaching out to get me.
My stomach was like a washing machine,
I felt bubbly inside.
In suspense watching it,
Round and round and round.
Fireworks going off in me,
Like Catherine wheels whizzing round in the sky.
As bubbly as a bee,
So wound up,
To go on *that* ride!
The excitement could not be controlled,
Like a knight going into battle,
Who would win?

Gemma Balestra (11)
Ball Green Primary School

ANGER

I could feel my anger about to explode,
I was so irritated,
My temper was getting hotter,
My head was burning up,
A fire spreading far,
What could I do?

I started to shout,
I felt rough and annoyed,
It was like a windstorm raging inside me,
As vicious as a snarling dog,
I stamped my feet and slammed the door,
What could I do?

Vicky Vardy (11)
Ball Green Primary School

SILENCE

What is silence?
Not a clock ticking, beating like your heart,
Not a dog barking, chasing a cat,
Not a kitten purring, cleaning its fur,
Not a squeaking bat flying around.
What is silence?
Not the trees swaying from side to side,
Not the wind whistling through the gnarled hands
of a tree,
Not the leaves rustling where a squirrel nestles,
Not a bird whistling, tweeting a merry tune.
What is silence?
Not children chuckling like cheeky monkeys,
Not tummies rumbling, waiting for their lunch,
Not teachers shouting or ranting and raving,
Not footsteps walking up and down.
What is silence?

Zoe Mellor (11)
Ball Green Primary School

ANGER

I could feel it growing in me, the anger was here.

My face started glowing red,
I stamped down the stairs like a herd of elephants.
The eyebrows over my eyes were shaped like a V,
I shouted 'I'm going out!' and slammed the door.
I was as angry as a bear hunting its prey.
I felt steamed up like a kettle,
My blood was boiling,
In my head I was saying, 'Get out of this mood,'
My eyes were fierce waves crashing upon rocky cliffs,
I felt like an exploding firework,
I needed help!

Melissa Gething (11)
Ball Green Primary School

THE SEA

The sea is a gentle kitten,
Softly and slowly rubbing against the rocks.
As it marks its territory,
It leaves the shore with a sign of life,
But as the sea gets sleepy and starts to shut its eyes,
It silently sneaks back and says goodnight.

As it becomes morning,
The sea pounces in,
To start again good and fresh
And bring the newness of the day.
But now the beach is open,
Children come and play
And now the waves are different,
In every kind of way.

But now the sea is an angry dog,
Grinding the rocks apart.
Waves crashing in and out,
Ripping the beach's very heart.
Scratching and biting, scars are left,
This is a ferocious event.

Charlotte Amison (11)
Ball Green Primary School

THE SEA

The sea is a gentle kitten,
Swaying up on the sandy bay.
As he comes, he lies on the beach
All the day.
As the sand blows,
He still goes.
As the wind roars,
He is licking his paws.
He climbs up a tree,
Like a tiger looking down at me.
He roars and roars,
Looking down at me with his terrible jaws.
I wait . . .

Stacey Snape (10)
Ball Green Primary School

SILENCE

Gentle breathing fills the air,
While the clock is softly ticking.

Lively girls chatter,
Like monkeys in a corner.

Footsteps running eagerly,
Down the corridor.

Squeaky chalk,
Upon the blackboard.

Children drowsy,
Feeling bored.

Is there ever peace and quiet?
I don't think so.

Becky Humphreys (10)
Ball Green Primary School

SILENCE

The shriek of a teacher you can hear in the hall,
All I can say is I don't like noise at all.
I hate noise!
The bang on the door that each child brings,
The phone in the office, it just rings and rings.
The quiet of a classroom, like a silent hushed moor.
It's the melody of brass from the room that's next door
And all I can say is that I hate noise!
When will it stop?
When will it end?
I hate noise!

Chelsie-Jo Payne (10)
Ball Green Primary School

SILENCE

I like silence but it never happens.
The clock ticking continuously,
A booming teacher warning a child to stop.
Footsteps from the headteacher coming to the classroom in a rage,
                                                a terrible rage.
A trombone and violin following a terrible tune,
Chalk screeching on the blackboard,
Children squabbling over a pencil,
Oh, what a sound, but I like silence.
A zip growling like a dog protecting its bone,
A pen rattling as someone silently writes,
Girls quarrelling in fury over a pink pen,
A chair scraping across the floor,
A person waffling about a question.
How bad can this get?

Marcus Robinson (10)
Ball Green Primary School

THE SEA

The sea is a gentle kitten,
So playful and calm.
The quiet waves,
Escape the rocks.

The sea gets angrier,
By the teasing wind.
She shows her white teeth
To anything that may get in her way.

The sea roars
Like an enormous tiger.
Crying out her warnings
To the ships in the night.

Stacey Butler (9)
Ball Green Primary School

WHY CAN'T I SLEEP?

When I am trying to sleep
I can hear my heart beat.
When I am trying to go to bed
I can hear ringing and banging in my head.
When I am trying to go to bed
I can hear things falling in my shed.
That's not all I can hear . . .
I can hear clocks ticking, the tap dripping,
People talking, walking and laughing.
I can hear bees buzzing, birds tweeting and flying,
Trees whistling, rain falling, my brother snoring,
My sister coughing, my dad shouting.
Why can't I sleep?

Gareth Jobburn (10)
Ball Green Primary School

SADNESS

I felt sadness inside me,
I couldn't hold on.
Someone had left me all alone,
My insides were unhappy,
Like someone breaking my heart.
I felt very mournful, like an animal hungry for food.

My body felt like cracking,
Like a chick out of an egg.
I was droopy,
Like a tree dying.
I looked out of my window,
Watching people go by.
My heart is full of sadness,
But I must face people in the end.

Lisa Condliffe (9)
Ball Green Primary School

SILENCE

I like silence,
Then the bell starts to ring,
Children are singing
And boys start to shout.
Teachers squawk.
I like silence.
Then girls start chattering,
I hate chalk screeching,
I like silence.
Pens scraping,
Pencils are rattling,
Pages flicking,
Doors that are banging.
Silence.
I like silence,
Then the noise starts again!

Leigh Gidman (10)
Ball Green Primary School

THE RIDE

The excitement couldn't be controlled,
The ride was just too *big!*
Like a steam train rushing through an empty tunnel,
Steam and smoke billowing out of its funnel.
It sped over the dumbstruck crowd,
The rumble of the ride was enormous!
Like a skateboard rushing down a hill,
Clashing and clattering as it comes.
The queue is getting smaller,
The ride lasts for just a second,
Nothing can slow it.
Loop-the-loop, loop-the-loop.
Nothing can stop it.
The excitement couldn't be controlled.
It's here!

Robert Wilshaw (10)
Ball Green Primary School

ANGER

I could feel it coming through my chest,
It burst out like a furious baboon.
My chest was going to explode,
Like a killing machine crushing.
I was a dog demolishing a bone.
My eyes exploded with water, like a volcano.
I was turning into a rampaging rhino.
I roared at everyone.
I was a shark in a frenzy.
My head was a snapping crocodile.
I was an evil spirit whooshing around.
I stirred wickedness around the room.
Where should I move to next?

Liam Stubbs (9)
Ball Green Primary School

THE SEA

The sea is a gentle kitten
Carefully washing its paws,
After rolling round
On sandy beach shores.

The sea is growing wild
The cat is getting rough,
All the white froth
Is really cat fluff.

He ran along the beaches
And across the golden sand.
Now he's going back again
Far from the land.

The sea is getting rougher now
Rougher than before.
The waves crash upon the beach
It's the tiger's paw.

Amy Martin (10)
Ball Green Primary School

ONE DAY

My boy's going to play for England,
I know he's good enough,
He's got the skill, he's got the speed,
And he's really tough.

At 6am we start to train,
Sunshine, snow, hail or rain,
We need to get him fit to play,
Because he'll play for England one day.

He runs, dribbles, passes, shoots,
Beckham's not fit to clean his boots,
At games I hear people say,
'I bet he'll play for England some day.'

On Sunday we polish the trophies he's won,
I know he'll make it to number one,
He's so sure he'll go all the way,
I know he'll play for England one day!

Ben Eardley (11)
Ball Green Primary School

SILENCE

The clock's ticking like the beat of a heart.
Wind howls like shadows of madness.
Chairs screeching like beamless demons.
Doors squeaking, begging for oil.
A child running down the corridor rapidly.
The doors banging, a sign that someone's mad.
The headteacher shouting on and on.
Aeroplanes rushing through the sky.
The horrible horns of traffic.
The world is never silent.

Sam Edwards (11)
Ball Green Primary School

ANGER

I've got a feeling steaming up my blood,
I've had an argument,
I can't cool down,
Anger like a dragon,
Shouting, screaming, pulling out hair,
Steam coming out of my ears,
My eyeballs are popping out,
I'm slamming doors,
Stamping feet like a rhino,
Launching off like a rocket,
Exploding!
When I breathe, I set things on fire,
It feels like I'm in a battle,
Don't come near me,
I'm dangerous,
I'm a dangerous weapon.
Watch out!

Matthew Pitchford (10)
Ball Green Primary School

ANGER

I could feel it growing
I could not stop it
Wickedness stirring around the room
I felt like a killing machine crushing its prey
My head was a raging storm
I was getting violent
A shark in a frenzy.

My face was a scrunched up newspaper
My head was about to explode
Eager to kill
Like a ferocious baboon
I was a rampaging rhino
A snapping crocodile
A savage creature ready and waiting to attack
Who would be next?

Dale Sheldon (9)
Ball Green Primary School

THE SEA

The sea is a sleepy kitten
purring with joy
swishing its tail side to side
like the waves

Beginning to roar
showing its teeth, the rocks
like razor blades can be fierce, can be calm.

Alice Moore (9)
Ball Green Primary School

TWO TIMES TWO IS FOUR

Two times two is four
I go on a secret tour.
Three times three is nine
We all have to stay in line.

Four times four is sixteen
I am really, really keen.
Five times five is twenty-five
I try hard to stay alive.

Six times six is thirty-six
I get myself into a fix.
Seven times seven is forty-nine
My hair looks really fine.

Eight times eight is sixty-four
I fall straight down to the floor.
Nine times nine is eighty-one
Joe had sweets and I had none!

Ten times ten makes one hundred
The running children's feet all thundered.
My rhyme now to you I tell
So you can learn your 'squares' as well.

Poppy Stott (9)
English Martyrs' Catholic Primary School

CHRISTMAS

The baby is coming
We are waiting
Waiting for our Saviour
Jesus Christ.

The baby is born
Shepherds arriving
With their sheep beside them
To see Jesus Christ.

The baby is crying
The wise men arriving
Following a shining star
To bring their gifts
To Jesus Christ.

Joe Stott (11)
English Martyrs' Catholic Primary School

CHRISTMAS

Angels are singing
Bells are ringing
Baby Jesus is here.

The shepherds are coming
With their sheep
To see the newborn King.

Wise men travelling
With their gifts:
Gold, frankincense and myrrh.

Chloe Hogan (10)
English Martyrs' Catholic Primary School

THE EAGLE

He flies the skies with crooked hands,
Close to sea over beautiful lands.
Above the azure world he stands,
He loves to live a simple life.

Robert Hunter (10)
English Martyrs' Catholic Primary School

FLUFFY

I love my little rabbit,
She really is quite nice.
She doesn't scratch you very much,
She's bitten me only twice!

My rabbit likes her carrot sticks,
She loves her nice warm toast,
But crunchy cream crackers,
It's those she loves the most.

She runs around the garden,
She eats all my mum's plants.
She never lets us catch her,
To her we're like giants!

It's time to go to bed now,
It's getting late at night.
I put my rabbit in her hutch,
My Fluffy, please sleep tight!

Chloe Horton (11)
English Martyrs' Catholic Primary School

THE HARBOUR

A beautiful harbour with all kinds of boats.
A charming building in the middle of the harbour.
The building has beautiful trees around it.
Birds fluttering and singing.
Trees swaying about in the breeze.
Delicious food in the restaurants.
Fresh, clean air all around.
Rocks under my feet and the sea on top of my toes.
The warm sun on my face.

Jessica Wright (8)
Greenways Primary School

HIGH MOUNTAINS

Snowy, frosted mountains in the autumn distant air,
Prickly trees with different coloured leaves,
Snowy bits of ice rolling down a mountain,
Trees swaying in the autumn breeze,
Bacon steam slowly floating out of black-roofed houses,
Scented emerald leaves,
A cool, gentle breeze running around me,
Grass wraps around my feet.

Daniel Brookes (8)
Greenways Primary School

THE SEASIDE VIEW

A pale, white bridge, with a boat silently floating in front,
High hills on the far horizon and a beautiful fruit tree,
Swishing and crashing waves against the swaying grass,
Crispy leaves crunching under my feet,
Salty sea water,
Pure, fresh air rushing past me,
Sun shining brightly on my face,
Water spraying on my body.

Yasmin Bailey (8)
Greenways Primary School

WINTER'S DAY

Frosted rings on a patterned, black, wooden gate,
A beautiful chapel with an arched doorway,
Evergreen trees, swaying in the winter breeze,
Crispy rustling leaves falling down to the ground,
Scented leaves whirling around the brick chapel,
Icy bushes with snowdrops on top,
Warm air spreading across my face,
The prickly trees rubbing against my legs.

Laura Mountford (9)
Greenways Primary School

OUT IN THE OPEN

Woolly sheep hungrily munching bracken on a hillside,
A lonely hill looming blue on the misty horizon,
Sheep bleating noisily in the fantastic countryside,
Fruit-bearing trees rustling in the spring breeze,
The scented purple heather that the sheep are eating,
The pure, fresh air slapping against my numb face,
The dewy grass brushing past my bare legs,
The woolly coat of a sheep tickling my legs,
I love it out in the open.

Callum O'Donnell (9)
Greenways Primary School

A WARM SUMMER'S MORNING

A beautiful rose garden all covered with richness
A cloudy, blue sky peering in the delicate T-shaped corner
The soft, gentle, blustery breeze
The shaking and rolling of the trees swaying and swirling
Fresh warmth with the sweet flowers
Poplars growing with caring texture
Silky flowers tickling my fingers
Lacy grass whirling around my feet.

Emily Cartlidge (8)
Greenways Primary School

THE CHURCH

On the floor there are some golden leaves,
A church with graves all around it,
Trees swaying in the gentle breeze,
People's feet coming by in this street,
Beautiful little flowers,
Candles that smell like fresh mint,
The breeze swaying by my head,
Leaves drifting down from the trees.

Reece Watts (9)
Greenways Primary School

MID MORNING

The sea multicoloured pink,
Buildings with a temple roof, with a pointed top,
Sea rushing from one side to the other,
Blackbirds squawking in the sky,
Beautiful fresh air with little bits of pink in the air,
The seaweed swishing in the sea,
Splinters in the wood,
The sea slipping through my fingers.

Bryony Tideswell (8)
Greenways Primary School

AN ANCIENT WINDMILL

An old, rickety windmill with tatty sails,
An ancient farmyard,
Birds singing as they flutter by,
The country breeze blowing in the wind,
The fresh air is whipping my face,
The silky flowers against my feet.

Alex Holt (9)
Greenways Primary School

SHIP CITY

Ships ready to sail on the salty sea,
Buildings standing like statues,
Human footsteps pounding on the ground,
The pine needles on the trees rustling,
The gentle breeze blowing up on the city,
The pavement skimming under my feet,
The boiling sun blazing on my face.

Benjamin Sharps (8)
Greenways Primary School

THE CHURCH

Fluffy white clouds in the pale blue sky,
A tall church in the far distance,
A magnificent lake at the side of the slippery grass,
Houses behind the tall waving trees,
A temple at the side of the tall church,
Small people walking behind the tall trees.

Zach Hind (9)
Greenways Primary School

THE RISING DRIFT

A dark sea with white boats sailing along in a row.
A lovely view of trees like a forest on a hilltop.
The rustling of the trees I can hear in the wind.
The clock on the tower ticking from left to right.
A lovely smell of trees.
The smell of clear and pure fresh air.
Gentle waves coming up to me as I dip my hand in.
The hot sun shining on my face warmly.

Larissa Panepinto (8)
Greenways Primary School

A DESERTED ISLAND

A deserted island with the long, tall pine trees peering over
the breezy water,
Some ducks swimming merrily along the bitterly cold lake,
Ducks quacking joyfully as they kick their legs underwater,
The wind whistling cheerfully as the scorching sun shines,
The smell of flowers in the fresh air,
The soft grass brushing my feet,
The wind blowing my face.

Frederick Jones (9)
Greenways Primary School

BOATS IN THE EVENING

The vibrant and glinting sun in the orange-lit sky,
Shadowy boats sailing on the ocean, then relaxing on dry land,
The gentle tides slashing the harbour's edge,
Orange-beaked seagulls signalling urgently to their mates,
The new wriggling yield of the hardworking fishermen,
Mineral salt in the flowing sea,
The shining rudder guiding its floating master,
Muddy land running through my dirty fingers.

Louise Wiggins (9)
Greenways Primary School

SNOWY MOUNTAINS

A cold, white, snowy mountain in the cloudy, misty air,
An imaginative picture of the fluffy, white cloud by the mountain,
Fresh air faintly blowing around me,
Green leaves on the trees rustling in the air,
Mountain freshness on the green, wild trees,
Fragile wind drifting in the air,
Cold bitterness of the frozen white snow,
Blue, calm, fragile wind in the drifty air.

Laura Hurst (9)
Greenways Primary School

MY BEAUTIFUL VIEW

Pure fruit dangling on spiky, delicate leaves,
Wide, strong buildings spreading out over rocky mountains,
Air briskly blowing over the enormous tall trees,
Huge trees rubbing against the magnificent buildings,
The fruit hanging on the high, long trees,
The clean fresh air,
A huge, cool mountain.

Alice Gething (9)
Greenways Primary School

FROSTING

Winding trees and the sugar-frosted branches upon them bending,
Snow-capped mountains with grassy bottoms,
Dropping icicles coming from twisted trees,
Wind briskly blowing the branches,
Music drifting from the church,
Footsteps from the church,
Leaves falling to the floor,
Breeze of frozen wings passing me,
The cold snow under my feet
Is making them freeze like icicles.

Philippa Bourne (8)
Greenways Primary School

SAILS ARE FLOATING BY

The bright blue reflecting sea on a sunny day,
Boats anchored in the deep, sparkling sea,
Fresh air blowing in the cloudless sky,
Sails flapping in the invisible, breezy wind,
Spicy food from wonderful restaurants,
Prickly, green trees swaying between the stalls,
The seawater freezing my fingers,
Warm, shining sun on my face.

Samuel Taylor (8)
Greenways Primary School

BEAUTIFUL WOOD

Trees that are bent and have broken branches,
Beautiful bluebells that dance in the wind,
Woodpeckers pecking at the wood in the trees,
The leaves fluttering in the trees,
Beautiful bluebells in the wood,
The fresh, clean breeze,
The wind blows through my hair,
The rough bark that belongs to the huge trees.

Michelle Beech (8)
Greenways Primary School

A SHALLOW FORD

A shallow water-splash runs across a cobblestone road
                             and under a stony bridge,
A bright blue sky is hovering over some lovely brick houses,
Bluebirds chirping and the cool wind whistling,
Trickling water from the ford,
Beautiful flowers in people's gardens,
Green pine trees towering over the dark, black road,
The water flowing across the lanes,
The gentle breeze on my face.

Jamie Cartlidge (8)
Greenways Primary School

LIFE IN THE ARCTIC

Blocks of frosty snow,
Cloudless blue sky,
Ice slides quickly into the magnificent ocean,
Snow melts softly in the lovely summer sun,
Pure, cool fresh air,
The coldness of the chilly ice,
The freezing breeze touching my face,
The cold snow freezing my feet.

Alex Burns (8)
Greenways Primary School

A MOTIONLESS WINDMILL

A motionless windmill in a field full of random colours,
An abandoned barn laying on an ancient farmyard,
A greedy crow nibbling at the golden corn,
A haunting noise in the creaking barn, that echoes all around,
Sweet scented flowers swaying in the breeze,
Cold country air flowing all around me,
Twitching grass tickling against my legs,
Hard dusty mud crunching as I walk.

Lucy Moston (9)
Greenways Primary School

ANCIENT WATER WHEELS

Two enormous ancient water wheels
Hanging onto old stone mills.
Bare trees hanging over the fast flowing river.
Birds are singing on the far horizon.
The pine trees are swaying gently in the cold breeze.
The pure clean fresh air is coming at my cool, chilled face.
The smoke of the blazing fire,
The warmth of the sun and it is blazing in my face.
The frosty white snow is tickling my ankle.

Jack Gibson (8)
Greenways Primary School

A WORLD WITHOUT WATER

No colourful rainbows
No hot shining sun
No refreshing rain
Nothing
It's all gone!

No green plants
No bright flowers
Dead flowers
Dead plants
Dead!
No nothing!

Jemma Ann Roberts (8)
Hanley St Lukes CE Aided Primary School

A WORLD WITHOUT WATER

No green grass
No fish pass
No rivers tinkling
No oceans bashing
Nothing!

Dying suns
Thirsty mums
Smelly feet
No laughter
Children crying
            crying
                mad!
No fun
No deserts
No baths

No bashing of the sea
No swishing of the sea
No splashing of the sea
No life!

Stephanie Crowley (8)
Hanley St Lukes CE Aided Primary School

A WORLD WITHOUT WATER

No green grass
No golden sun
No colourful rainbows
Nothing!
There's nothing!
No
    People
No
    World.

Jack Parsons (8)
Hanley St Lukes CE Aided Primary School

A WORLD WITHOUT WATER

No life
No ice
Dying sun
A dying world

Burning
Boiling
Scalding
World

No gardens
No ponds
No beaches
No oceans
No water

Dirty
Smelly
Bodies
And feet

No . . . nothing!

Halil Edward Eren (8)
Hanley St Lukes CE Aided Primary School

A WORLD WITHOUT WATER

Brown dry grass
Cracking Earth everywhere
No swimming baths
No children smiling again
Animals thirsty for water
No garden ponds
Everything hot!

Hot!
Hot!
Hotter!
Now nothing!

William Wainwright (8)
Hanley St Lukes CE Aided Primary School

PAT

We looked outside in our yard,
Dad said 'Look! It's raining hard!'
Outside we went and Rosie said 'Stop! What's that?'
Dad said 'Pat' or something like that.
Pat saw us and ran away
To live for another day.

It was the following morning,
Rosie looked out yawning,
'Pat is back!' Rosie told Dad
He said 'Don't worry, that's not bad!'
We opened the door and the rain began to pour
Pat again ran away,
To live for yet another day.

Rosie Mayer (9)
Hanley St Lukes CE Aided Primary School

RYAN'S CHRISTMAS POEM

When the children sleep
Santa comes along
Happiness the children keep
Children praise with a song.

Exciting isn't it?
People having fun
Maybe wearing a Santa kit
Presents weigh a tonne.

Happiness is all around us
Sing happy songs,
People riding a bus and
The bells going ding dong.

Ryan Lawrence (9)
Hanley St Lukes CE Aided Primary School

LIGHT

Mum turns the light off
The shadows start to loom
I pull the quilt over my head
They're all around my room.
Big ones, small ones, scary ones too.
I'm sure there are Gremlins under my bed
Oh what am I going to do?
But as the light flows through the door
It's just my mum coming to kiss me
I look all around my room, there's
nothing there at all.
I give myself a little smile
And to sleep I start to fall.

Ryan Malbon (11)
Hanley St Lukes CE Aided Primary School

AUTUMN

Leaves fall
  Harvest is here
    Animals hibernate
      Leaves fall on the ground at
      Autumn
        Autumn's here

        Summertime
         Hot sun
           Blazing brightly
             Yellow, red and orange
             Children swimming
           Sea
           All day.

Amy Watts (10)
Hanley St Lukes CE Aided Primary School

WINTER POEM

A chill in the air
But what do I care?
As the grounds all a-glow
With gleaming white snow

It's a beautiful sight to be seen
All the streets looking so bright and clean
With Christmas lights shining so bright
All through the cold winter's night

Winter is one of my favourite seasons
For all sorts of reasons
But especially for Christmas, with the laughter and fun
A happy time for everyone!

Jodie Miller (10)
Hanley St Lukes CE Aided Primary School

MY BROTHER

My brother, he is very small,
He screams and screams and screams,
He gives me such a headache
He's even in my dreams

My brother, he is very small
He cries and cries and cries,
Sometimes he creeps up quietly
And gives me a surprise.

My brother, he is very small
He laughs and laughs and laughs,
He tickles me and tickles me,
And sometimes makes me gasp.

My brother, he is very small,
I love him very much, but sometimes
I wish that he was a
White rabbit in a hutch.

Jade Moore (10)
Hanley St Lukes CE Aided Primary School

CHRISTMAS POEM

Winter is white with snow,
Children shine with a healthy glow.
It's a time to be jolly
Making wreaths of Christmas holly.

Presents, trees and decorations,
Parties with our relations.
Kisses under the mistletoe,
Hoping no one has to go.

Baby Jesus, born this day,
Lay in a cradle made of hay.
Christmas is a time to say
'We love you Jesus,
Please don't go away.'

Natasha Chesters (10)
Hanley St Lukes CE Aided Primary School

DARK

There's no more light
It's time for night
I see fireworks in the dark
I see fireflies in the park
I miss the bright day
There's a horse in the hay
It's gone quiet, not even a bleep
Then I fall asleep.

Tiffany Allen (11)
Hanley St Lukes CE Aided Primary School

WINTERTIME

Winter comes once a year
In the snow lots of children play.
The frost clings onto everybody's cars,
Children go out to play on their sledges.
Lots of people look forward to winter coming,
Robins sit in the trees, singing a beautiful song.
The snow is very, very beautiful.
When the sun shines, it melts all the snow.
When it snows, it blows a cold wind,
The snow makes the river's water turn to ice.
People like to make their footprints in the snow,
The frost hangs on to hedges and houses.

Ruth Boughey (11)
St Saviour's CE Primary School

WINTER DAYS

Winter's here! Winter's here!
The wind's too cold, I hear
It only comes once a year
Come on, get up! The snow is here.

It is cold outside, it's warm inside
Your nose and cheeks glow up.
It looks like a blanket,
Footprints in the snow, go everywhere
And leave marks.

Is it glitter in the snow?
What is it I hear?
Soon the sun will come back out
And the snow will disappear
It will be gone!

Kirsty Brookes (10)
St Saviour's CE Primary School

WINTER

Winter is bitter and *cold!*
I go out and see little pawprints in the snow.
I play snowballs in the snow.

Four season cats. Tonight's winter.
Summer, autumn and spring.
Asleep, waiting to awaken.

I wish it would last,
So I could build a snowman!
The plants look dead, but they aren't!
Children are playing in the snow, having fun.

Kerry Lacey (10)
St Saviour's CE Primary School

WINTER

Sparkling white
Frost bites
Icicles hang from houses
Children sliding -
On ice.
Cars are skidding
Snowmen built,
Children throwing snowballs
Winter's cold!
Winter comes once a year
People are cold
People stay in bed!

John Lacey (10)
St Saviour's CE Primary School

WAR

Through the trenches, bent backs, stand
Listening to people crying and dying.
Hitler speaks and Germany fight.
'Let's go and kill those Brits!'
That's what the Germans shout.

Soldiers destroying each persons life
But they don't care as long as they win.
Relatives crying, dreading the postman,
Coming to their house with a brown envelope
Explosives go bang, and people die.

Gas leaks -
Soldiers run,
But there's always one who doesn't make it
To get out of the building.

Kyle Batty (10)
St Saviour's CE Primary School

SNOW LAND

A wind, cold, blowy
and sometimes very snowy.

The snow glistens in the sun
when the children are having fun.

Snowball fights, that's what people like!
With a cup of hot chocolate with marshmallow balls.

But the thing I like best is
The sunlight on the sparkling white.

It's just like a snow land!

Liam Barton (10)
St Saviour's CE Primary School

SEASONS

Summer suns are very bright and beautiful,
Winter is cold, damp and pitiful,
Autumn, and leaves twirl on the ground,
Spring is when baby animals are born.

Summer is hot and bright,
It's a nice world.

Autumn is cold and trees lose their leaves,
They scatter over the ground.

Winter is snowy and rainy,
It makes your toes tingle.

Spring is when flowers appear,
To brighten up the world.

Craig Anchors (10)
St Saviour's CE Primary School

THAT'S WINTERTIME

Snow falling on the ground
Falling, falling without a sound.
The winter is bitter and rough
Fields full of snow
Cars covered in frost
That's wintertime!

Beautiful sparkling snow
Gardens covered in snow
I love to make the first footsteps in it
I love to hear the robin sing.
He sits waiting for the spring
That's wintertime!

I love wintertime
It's the best season.

Daniella Savage (10)
St Saviour's CE Primary School

WINTER

Snow falls to the ground
The robins making a beautiful sound
The children all wrapped up warm.
Building a snowman with hopes that it wouldn't melt!
The snowman had two pieces of coal for eyes,
He hopes that it doesn't fry.
The wind is getting colder and more bitter
The treetops are full with glitter.
On the grounds it's like sheets of white.
The icicles hanging on the roof,
The snow is nearly waterproof,
My brother's wrapped up warm.
With a hat, scarf and much, much more.
The frost is clinging to the fence
But the view of snow is the most beautiful sight of the year.
Winter is my favourite season.

Samantha Tokely (10)
St Saviour's CE Primary School

CRUEL WINTER

Winter is cold, dull and miserable
Clouds are full with snow.
I love making footsteps in the snow
I feel low, I don't know why?
I get frostbite,
I want to stay in bed
I'll probably be ill
Because I got a chill.

Ami Hamnett (11)
St Saviour's CE Primary School

DOLPHINS

Jump, twist, splash
Up go the dolphins.
Passing seaweed to each other
From their fins.

'Pass the seaweed'
Is a game they play
That way, this way
They pass it to each other,
They play it in groups, all day.

Sneaking, swimming,
Under the water
Mother dolphins always love
And look after their
Son or daughter.

Light grey, dark grey, grey
These are the colours of dolphins
They even come in white.
If they get lost they
Follow the stars at night.

Jennifer Aynsley (11)
St Saviour's CE Primary School

WINTER THOUGHTS

Winter is dark, dreary and cold
The leaves are crumpled, crinkled and old.
Frost is all over people's ledges,
And stuck to the tall wide hedges.
Spiderwebs glistening, glittering bright
The snow stands out in the night.
Little footprints in the snow,
Different animals come and go.
Frost stays stuck to car windscreens.
All the snow gives beautiful scenes,
Snow is beautiful, winter is cold,
Winter can be dull, dreary and bold!

Chelsey Birt (11)
St Saviour's CE Primary School

SHINE OH SUN

When I wake up in the morning,
I stretch up high.
I look out of the window
Shine, oh sun, shine.

I walk down the stairs
Then eat my breakfast.
I walk to the window
Shine, oh sun, shine.

At night-time, just before
I get into my bed,
I think tomorrow, sun oh sun,
Shine, oh sun, shine.

Nicole Locker (10)
St Saviour's CE Primary School

WHAT IS WAR FOR?

What is war for?
People are leaving their homes
They might not even come back
To their own front doors.
It's just people, wasting their lives.

They go in planes to get ready to fly,
But soon their planes get blown up and they die!
The people's relatives don't know what is happening
But the people in the war are going to die.

I don't know what war's for
I can't believe what is happening
What is war for?

Ben Giddy (11)
St Saviour's CE Primary School

FIREWORKS

They go straight up into the air
Then it goes *bang!*
Colours light up the sky
Catherine wheels, spinning really fast.

They crackle and sizzle,
Dogs start to bark and then become scared.
Then an air bomb flashes
And everyone cheers.

The smell of burgers and hot dogs cooking,
And the sizzling of the bonfire.
As everyone enjoys themselves,
Watching, watching the colourful sky.

Vicky Faulkner (10)
St Saviour's CE Primary School

WINTER

Snow on the treetops sparkling in the light,
Snowmen with their black hats and coal eyes and noses.
Puddles turn to ice, ponds freeze.
Frost on the window screens.
Snow covers everything in sight,
Birds fly away to warmer countries
Icicles drop off buildings and people dodge them
Children are happy, having snowball fights.
Then suddenly, it starts to go all slushy
It starts to get a little warmer every day.
The puddles start to go all mushy, the pond ice
Cracks easily,
The ice melts and the children are unhappy.

Thomas Boulton (11)
St Saviour's CE Primary School

ONE DAY OUT FISHING

I was fishing at a lake
The lake was big and
I was small
My float was bobbing up and down
I was sitting in my chair.
My float went down
I shot up and struck my rod.
There was nothing on my hook!
Except a half-dead maggot!
I went into my pack
I got a bacon sandwich
I took a bite of my sandwich
My float went under
I struck my rod.
So very quickly, on the end was a fish
So small!
It was a baby roach and
I put it straight back in.
I set my rod again
I didn't have a bite all day long
So I packed my things away
And I set off for home.

Adrian Lovatt (11)
St Saviour's CE Primary School

IT'S WINTER

Sledding down the bank we go
People falling on their bums
Winter is really frosty
Winter is really nasty!
People sniffing
People feel really cold
Everywhere is white.
We all hope winter goes.
Children playing in the snow,
Children building snowmen.
People laughing and joking
Everywhere I go
Tucked in bed, warm at last.

Amy Mould (10)
St Saviour's CE Primary School

ARE TEACHERS WHAT THEY SEEM?

'Are teachers what they seem?'
I hear you all yell out.
Do they really like it?
When we make them scream and shout.

Well I'll let you into a secret
My teacher's not like that.
To be really truthful
She lets us talk and chat. (I wish!)

I don't see why she's different
She just doesn't seem quite right
She must really love her job,
Because she works until ten at night.

When we are all quiet
The headteacher comes in,
He brings her a cup of coffee
And a filled up biscuit tin. (*She wishes!*)

Mrs Gratton is a good teacher
The girls think she's funny,
She isn't that bad,
But the lads think she's mad.

Ashleigh Hampson (10)
St Saviour's CE Primary School

IT'S WINTER

Winter's cold, frost and blowing wind,
Frost is over there and all over the hill.
White sparkling snow, so, so, wonderful.
Weeds wither, ready to live again,
It's beautiful, so beautiful.
It's nearly all gone and make the most of it
It's so cold, dull and grey,
With a moaning wind.
Lots of days left
With a lovely look.
I love winter, winter is great.
Oh, I love winter!

Matthew Viggars (10)
St Saviour's CE Primary School

WINTER

Winter is bitter
Winter is cold
Winter is here
But will soon go.

I love winter
I love the snow
But I don't like it
When it goes.

Snow falls gently
Onto the ground
When the sun comes back
It will all melt down.

You see red cheeks
And red noses,
Cold hands
And cold toes.

Lindsey Adewumi (10)
St Saviour's CE Primary School

BONFIRE NIGHT

Suddenly in this cold, dark night
A firework shoots and all is alight,
When they burst, it's like a flower
And then they fall in a shower.

Flames roar high,
High in the sky.
They eat everything in their way
I wish Bonfire Night was every day!

The fireworks go bang, bang, bang
'Remember, remember' the children sang.
Rockets fly with a zoom, zoom, zoom
Every second is a big boom, boom!

Make sure you keep your pets inside
Until morning and everything has died.
All the bangs have disappeared
With no bangs, it seems all weird!

Not many people remember the story
King James was lucky, it could have been gory.
Guy Fawkes was executed and paid his price
You wouldn't want to see it, it wasn't nice!
                                Honestly!

Ryan Wilson (10)
St Saviour's CE Primary School

BONFIRE NIGHT

Bang, bang, bang
There they go like rockets
All the colours splurting out
Bonfires crackling, crackling
The smell from the food.

The night goes on
Bang, bang, bang
Fireworks like shooting stars
The night goes on,
Colours that fall into rain
Bang, bang, bang!

Kim Moore (11)
St Saviour's CE Primary School

THE LISTENER - A SEQUEL

Traveller and steed galloped through the gloomy forest,
Where the black bats swooped down.
Crying voices whimpered in the coldness of the wind,
Owls stared at the traveller with a frown.
Hearing strange voices coming from the trees,
Grass slowly swirled in the frosty wind
Was there anybody there, around the breeze?

Helen Wood (10) & Kimberley Withington (11)
St Thomas' RC Primary School

THE ATTIC

Stepping up the sturdy ladders
Into the treasure trove of history.
Cobwebs dangled from rafters,
Peeping into one of the ancient chests
I found the most beautiful dress.
It was my mother's wedding dress.
I lifted it up,
My father's suit was revealed underneath
Folded lovingly.
Fragments of light crept in
Through the cracked tiles
Onto furniture
Longing for the day to be used again.

Steven James (11)
St Thomas' RC Primary School

HIDDEN TREASURE

I see only my hidden treasure
That no one else knows about.
But if you sit quietly
You will find out.

The gloomy corners of the attic are forests' mouths
Ready to devour anything that stands in their way.
Shimmers of patient light haunt it,
Is this my hidden treasure . . . no!

Moth-eaten dresses which have been there for years
Stand proud and tall, as memories flow like a gushing river
Before my troubled eyes.

Torn teddy bears watching, waiting
For someone to rescue them.
Peering through the window
Graceful beams of light.
From a thin young lady in a gleaming glistening gown
And cloak of silver with imprinted moonlit stars.

As far as the eye can see.

Silky cobwebs enwrap my feelings, feelings of excitement.
A voice says 'This is your life.'
'Who is it?' I shout, as the room fills with silence.

Suddenly a fragmented shiver trickles down my spine
For something is going to happen.
Is it my hidden treasure?

I believe it is
The graceful lady
We have been friends for years.
She says it is time to part,
She smiles, thins out, body then face, and is gone.

Hannah Smith (10)
St Thomas' RC Primary School

THE ATTIC

Cobwebs trickled from the sturdy rafters
Walls crumbled with age
Gloomy fragments of light peer through the window
Books tattered and ripped thrown in a cold, wet box
Old toys, waiting to be played with
Curtains thrown over boxes, wanting to be used
Moth-eaten clothes sharing happier times
Photographs bringing back long-forgotten memories
Furniture, longing for the day it will be used again
Papers faded with dampness and cold.
Wine and whisky bottles covered with thick layers of dust
Clocks not working
Cold dampness making things soggy
Can't bear to throw anything away!
Just keep it up in the attic.

Thomas Wilcox (11)
St Thomas' RC Primary School

TILL THE END

I reach up for the moon, till my fingers can stretch no further,
Tired of reaching, I entwine my arms to keep my body warm,
Whilst the winter snow settles on my bushy hair.
My long feet gently dab the pond nearby.
I can talk to the friendly stars, whilst they sing me to sleep
With their lullaby.
On the distant horizon, what is that I see?
Is it a red bush? Oh no, a fire is rushing towards me.
The temperature rises. I get too hot,
I flap my arms to keep myself cool.
The fire reaches me, I frantically wave my arms,
I splash my feet in the pond, as the water catches the fire.
It whimpers, I beat it, but no one was there to see me.
I could tell them
I fought till the end.

James Durrant (10)
St Thomas' RC Primary School

ATTIC

An icy shiver
Tingling my spine
As I tiptoe into
The enchanted attic

Mist creeping up through rafters
Interlacing its body,
Noses trickling fingers of silver cobwebs.

Toys lying motionless
A blanket of thickening hair
Growing over them, day by day.

Shadowy darkness enwrapping me
In its velvet hand.

Crystals hanging from dresses
Catch the moon's radiant light,
Like the sun on a glacier.

Walls who used to be mighty
Giants are now crumbling in misery

Books faintly humming;
Bursting with imagination
And excitement, fighting to get out.

Gazing at all the wonders of this attic,
A magic box with desirable dreams,
Longing for the rusty lock to break . . .

Anastasia Donaldson (11)
St Thomas' RC Primary School

THE ATTIC

Dark spooky attic
Cobwebs
Hanging in every corner
Old, crinkled, brown, tattered teddy.
Leaning on crumbling walls,
Precious velvet christening shoes,
Boxed tenderly. Memorable birthday cards,
Fitting gently to one corner
Dirty clothes
Piled neatly leaning on the coloured
Teddies and dolls.
Loved to bits,
Sitting by a pile of books.
Last of all reminders
A wedding dress
Wrapped in tissue paper.
It wasn't so spooky after all!

Rosanna Rapacchietta (10)
St Thomas' RC Primary School

INTO THE ATTIC

As I stepped into the attic
A small eerie shiver crept up my spine.
A pile of old crumpled-up papers lay there,
In a layer of dust, waiting to be read.
The moon's silkiness seeped
Through each broken pane of the window.

There it was . . .
The chest.
An aged rusty lock, kept it tightly closed.
The key? It was hidden underneath.
I opened it
My childhood dreams enwrapped me in my feelings.
Feelings of the past.
Toys, books and many more things lay there sleeping
Unharmed.

I turned back
The walls,
Which used to be the highlight of the room
Were now the misery.
Beautiful hung-up clothes let their colours fade
As they waited to be touched once again
Looking up
I saw cobwebs trickling from mossy rafters
As spiders looked overhead.

All my childhood dreams were awaiting me in my mind,
I had found the hidden treasure.
My life.

Sarah Downie (11)
St Thomas' RC Primary School

THE WINTER TO REMEMBER

I stood there, proud and tall on the hill, alone and cold.
Rubbing my leaves and curling in my branches,
I looked for the stars
And in the dark blackness of that winter's evening.
In the middle of the bleakness, I saw the stars.
In the moonlight they danced round the moon,
For a moment I felt a strange sensation,
I bowed my head and found the ground was frosty underfoot,
And I heard something crackling far in the distance.
I stood straight and firm.
What was it?
I couldn't see
Then I noticed . . . there it was
Blazing far beyond the meadow gate
Saw it . . . it moved
It started drawing closer
And I smelled the smoke on the winter air.
A state of panic I could feel
What to do?
I could not move
As it burned closer leaving a smouldering trail.
I prayed to God . . . hoped He'd save me
And He did
It poured with rain, before it had reached the meadow gate.

Daniel Scragg (11)
St Thomas' RC Primary School

HIDDEN TREASURES

I thought about last night
In my bed, so warm
When I was so little
And my blankets so torn.
That day I went up
Where I hadn't been before.
So gloomy and misty and filled with treasures,
I saw something in the corner
Glistening in the dark.
I went to see what it was
A picture frame, I think.
I'll go and tell my mum.
She's as happy as can be
To see what I've found.
She's really happy with me.

Sarah Thorley (10)
St Thomas' RC Primary School

COIN COLLECTION

Creak, creak, creak
The stairs creak as I walk.
The old broken door slowly opens.

The old attic isn't safe,
I almost fall down a hole!
I see a very old box
Should I open it?

I walk towards the box
And I open it. I close it and I open it again.
The lid lies there, lonely.

Money! Money! Lots of money.
One shilling, half a crown, sixpence,
Tuppence and a one pound note!

Does Mum know? I bet she doesn't!
This shows what money Grandad had.
Should I tell her?

Thomas Rowley (9)
St Thomas' RC Primary School

Hidden Treasure

Dig, dig, dig . . . then bump!
My spade had hit an old chest,
I opened it frantically.
I started taking out the contents.
Then I realised it was cloth,
But at the very bottom there was a diary.
In big loopy writing, I had never seen before, it read
'Grandpa'.
I could have danced with joy
Because I had found a book about
My grandpa.

Alexander Jones (9)
St Thomas' RC Primary School

HIDDEN TREASURE

In my nana's attic,
I saw something twinkling and bright.
So I went to see what it was,
I rejoiced, it was hidden treasure!

I played and messed about a bit,
After I ran and jumped about everywhere.
I tried to keep the treasure secret,
I hid it from everyone.

I took some of it, small pieces though,
People would get suspicious.
Then it was gone,
I'd spent it all.

Martin Regan (9)
St Thomas' RC Primary School

THE TREASURE UNDER THE SEA

The sea was dark and blue
The dolphins sprung at me from time to time,
As my mum spoke, birds flew over us listening.
My nan spoke,
'Under the dark waters there is a hidden diary
it tells a story of the past.'
I watched as she disappeared into the mist
The days went by and I thought that is it
I ran and ran
Before I knew it, I was in the sea,
There it was, the diary
But sshh! It's a secret!

Josephine Lasota (9)
St Thomas' RC Primary School

MY LOVING SISTER KATE

She looks like a beautiful model
Her hands are like warm leaves,
Her face is like a lovely peach
She has eyes like a gorgeous dolphin.
Her clothes are pretty like princess' dresses
She moves like a baby bear
She walks like a cute guinea pig
She runs like a mouse
Kate thinks she is a disco diva!

I think she's the nicest sister in the world.

Philippa Plant (8)
St Thomas' RC Primary School

MY BEST FRIEND'S BABY

They said they'd let me hold her
In the living room.

She was cute and beautiful
With her loving smile.

She was warm and cuddly and
She wasn't heavy at all.

I felt really special and happy
I hope I'll hold her again
Sometime.

Lisa Dawson (9)
St Thomas' RC Primary School

HIDDEN TREASURE

Deep, deep beneath the ocean waves
Where there are lots of sand and shells
There's a deep dark secret
Which I cannot tell.

All the creatures live down there,
Like crabs, lobsters and fish
They keep the secret intact
But I'll tell you if you wish.

There's treasure under the ocean
Which is protected by them all,
And if there's any trouble near
Then the seals start to call.

Then all the sharks came darting
Altogether like a team
And the divers quickly swim away
With a high-pitched scream!

Then the mermaids, fish and dolphin
The lobsters, crabs and the rest
All start laughing at the diver
And how they protected the chest.

So if you see something shining
And you wonder what is there,
Keep your curiosity to yourself
Or you'll surely have a scare!

Amy Watkin (11)
Smallthorne Primary School

HIDDEN TREASURES

Underneath the ocean waves
Where the fish swim with fear,
Of being eaten by a shark
There is something else coming near.

A head filled with memories
Of family, friends and jokes.
Between the stones and seaweed
And a pile of old bicycle spokes.

Shoals of dolphins and fish swim by
All unaware
Of something lurking in the shadows
Swimming over there.

A diver seeking treasure
Diamonds, rings and jewels,
He searches in the depths of the sea
And in rocky pools.

Laura Cartwright (11)
Smallthorne Primary School

HIDDEN TREASURE

Deep, deep down
At the bottom of the ocean
Lying under the sand
Never been opened.

Deep, deep down
A muddy box is stored
Loaded with treasure
Far beyond the shore.

Deep, deep down
Not a sight to be seen,
For no one knows
Of the pleasant dream.

Roxanne Bradshaw (10)
Smallthorne Primary School

TREASURE HUNT

In search of treasure
They sailed the seas,
From north to south, from east to west
In search of the family treasure chest.

They came upon an island, so small and hidden,
They thought to go there would be forbidden,
They dared to walk upon the land
Where they saw diamonds gleaming in the sand.

Amongst the seaweed and the shells,
They found more jewels and golden bells,
Rubies red and diamond rings
This made them all into kings.

Nicola Glaze (11)
Smallthorne Primary School

THE WHALE

Sea waving, sea glistening
Sea hiding all the gifts
Whales dancing, whales jumping
So happily he drifts

He rides on the ocean
Like a king so free
I love them, I love them
How I wish it could be me.

Annabel Shenton (8)
The Faber RC Primary School

FATHER CHRISTMAS

In the North Pole lives Father Christmas,
His friends the elves are making the toys
For the girls and boys themselves.
Father Christmas goes outside to
Feed his reindeer, cat and dog.
After that he sets off on his sleigh,
The reindeer's bells ring in the night sky.
Father Christmas is busy down the chimney.
He is putting the presents under the tree for Lizzy
Father Christmas eats the mince pies,
Then gets back on his sleigh and on his way.
Father Christmas flies up in the sky,
On his way from house to house
The bells ring, jing, jing, jing.
The reindeer walk up in the sky,
From house to house they fly.
The stars are bright like twinkling lights,
Rudolph has his nose so bright.
So he can guide the sleigh tonight.
All at once Father Christmas, flies around the world,
He stops just once and the job is done.
He's had a lot of fun,
That's because he's magic!
Thank you Father Christmas
From everyone!

Naomi Tyers (7)
The Faber RC Primary School

REAL

Giants aren't real
But in the mind, they are.
Helicopters are real,
I've never seen one, have you?
Cats are real,
I have seen one of those.
Because some of my friends
Have got one as a pet.
Caves are real
Because I've seen one once.

Elizabeth Thrush (7)
The Faber RC Primary School

Cows

My grandad has some Highland cows, which are very ugly,
He keeps them in fields, which are sometimes very boggy.
He keeps the bull in the shed, with a bed made of hay
And that is where he is going to stay till spring.
They kick a lot and drink a lot, out of a very large pot,
They are very dangerous and heavy.
Their hair is thick and long which makes them very hairy,
They have very big horns, which makes them look very scary.

Harry Mellor (8)
The Faber RC Primary School

FIRE

I like fire.
I like the colours,
Red, yellow, orange and blue.
I like the sound fire makes,
Pop, bang, crackle and fizz.
I like the shapes
The fire makes,
Swervy, curly dragon shapes.

Thomas Goodwin (8)
The Faber RC Primary School

SPRINGTIME

The crocuses and snowdrops are pushing through the ground,
The frost and snow have disappeared and spring is all around.

The fields are looking greener, the trees are budding too.
And in-between the fluffy clouds, the sun is peeping through.

I listen in the morning, to birdsong on the air,
The signs that spring is really here are showing everywhere.

My favourite time is springtime, the wintry days are through,
The whole world seems a happier place, with lots to look forward to.

Isaac Cooke (9)
The Faber RC Primary School

HIDDEN TREASURES

I went to open the trunk
but I didn't like the clunk.
I heard a sound
but it was all a nice sound.

I said 'What's that?'
But it was just a cat.
It was a black cat
so I called it Pat.

When I got it out of the ground,
it made a sound.
The necklaces were golden
but when I looked, they just looked
as though they had been stolen.

When we went back, the light started to fade
so I had a drink of Lucozade.

Beverley Rushton (8)
The Faber RC Primary School

WHEN I RODE A HORSE

On the 30th of August 2001
I went horse riding
My friend and I loved it.
The horse went nice and steady
But my mum's kept on jumping
When Mum took us again
We all had jumping horses and
None of us liked that one.
The horse made a sound like this . . .
Clip-clop!

Michelle Barleyman (9)
The Faber RC Primary School

PADDY UPSTAIRS, JOHNNIE DOWNSTAIRS, MY FRIENDS

Johnnie downstairs runs the shop,
Paddy upstairs runs the restaurant.

Johnnie downstairs has a house,
Paddy upstairs has a bungalow.

Johnnie downstairs drives a van,
Paddy upstairs rides a bike,
Sometimes they swap.

Johnnie downstairs has a brother,
Paddy upstairs has a brother,
They are brother to each other.

Callum McGuire (9)
The Faber RC Primary School

SPORT

Sport, where do we feel it?
The atmosphere of the game is amazing.
The cheer of the crowd,
The swing of the bat,
The kick of the ball,
The throwing of the ball.
A sudden change of the score.
The liveliness in the people,
The excitement of the crowd, the game,
The world outside the stadium.
Wham! The ball is in the net.
Whack! The racquet hits the ball.
Whoosh! The crowd are cheering.
Wow! Sport.
It makes me dream!

Harriet Collier (10)
The Faber RC Primary School

ROCKETS

The rocket's engine's on,
Five, four, three, two, one.
The rocket's in space,
And looks out of place.
While going to the moon,
While going to the moon.

It flies past stars,
A lot faster than cars.
The stars are big and round,
It's more fun than on the ground.
While going to the moon,
While going to the moon.

The rocket's landing soon,
And it makes a big *boom!*
The moon buggy's out,
And trundling about.
While on the moon,
While on the moon.

Kate Hargreaves-Brough (9)
The Faber RC Primary School

SPORTS

Football is a sport
Where the ball is passed,
Trying to score the goal
As the crowd roar.

Skateboarding is a sport,
As the riders do their stunts.
Backflips, 180s and Rack and Rolls,
To the fast 900.

Racing is a sport
With cars and motorbikes,
As they race to the finish,
Where the chequered flag is drawn.

Tennis is a sport,
Where you keep the ball spinning.
15 love, 30 love,
Until it's over, game, set and match.

Jonathan Ball (11)
The Faber RC Primary School

KATY THE DOG

Katy the dog is naughty and very playful too.
She chases me and Harry and chews on Daddy's shoe.
She likes to go for walks and likes to hold the lead
She likes to try and tug us, till we're tumbling off our feet.
She likes to chase the cat and bark at her a lot
She's always very hungry and likes to have her treats
She's always very friendly to everyone she meets.

Samuel Mellor (10)
The Faber RC Primary School

UNTITLED

Just dream a little dreamer,
You've gotta seem so much keener.
Close your eyes and off you go,
All the way to Mexico!
Cos that's what dreams can do,
You never know what's coming to you.
You can dream of this, I can dream of that,
Now, do you know what I'm getting at?
Dreams can come true,
Expect it just out of the blue.
Dreams are shocking, surprising,
And even scary!
With monsters just too hairy.
And then comes the nice dreams,
With woodland walks and country talks.
Dreams are like snowflakes,
Each one separate and unique.
Never, ever pass one by,
Because soon the dreamy wish . . .
                    . . . will die!

Rosie Shenton (10)
The Faber RC Primary School

SPACE THROUGHOUT

Throughout space,
Everything is a challenge.
Surviving through the stars and planets,
Very fast and bright shooting stars
Go around the other planets and Mars.
Jupiter is a hot gas with a hot burn
Saturn is on a slight turn.
Pluto with the looks of cold,
Uranus that looks round and bold.
The moon that shines at night,
And the sun that shines with light.
The Earth turns all of the time
With clouds over the land.
Mercury is gas that looks like sand.
Planet Venus that's green land
With poison in the air,
Comets fly through the air
While people stare.
The solar system is bright and wide.
Black holes that are moving on their side.

Matthew Brindley (10)
The Faber RC Primary School

THE VIEW FROM MY ROOM

As I looked out of my window
The snow was like dough
I asked if I could go out
Mum said, 'Wrap up tight!'
Thomas came out to play
'Come on Chris, it's a great day!'

We had a great idea
And with some cheer
'Igloo that's what we'll build'
'Come on Chris, stop us being chilled.'
The snow was deeper by the hour
Trying to build our large tower.

All that night I looked out,
From my room, what a delight
To see our creation
Shine in the light,
As I looked down the very next day
Our great tower had almost gone away.

Christopher Rushton (11)
The Faber RC Primary School

SAMMY

I have a dog named Sammy
His paws are so big and clammy
His tail is long
His ears are flappy
And he acts a little bit batty.
His coat is shiny and black
His eyes are big and brown
He runs like the wind and does mischievous things
Until he hears you shout, *'Biscuit!'*

Jack Harvey (8)
The Richard Heathcote CP School

I AM A TREE

At the start of the year I am born,
As a little seed I grow.
Put me in the soil
I grow into a shoot
But this is only the start of the year in spring.

It's the summer now the spring has gone,
I grow into a sapling.
But I have no clue as to what I am.
It's my childhood days
I am growing still.

Autumn is when my leaves fall off
And I now know what I am
I am a beech tree
Tall and strong
No man can cut me down.

It's winter now
I'm old, no one wants me
All my seeds are falling off
As I am dragged to a truck.
I am dead but my babes will live
They are going to grow and die
But we'll live on
Forever!

Cherie Watson (11)
The Richard Heathcote CP School

THE GENTLE NIGHT

The night has a lovely face,
And is set in a lovely place.
It is gentle and calming,
It is sweet and snug.
When the night starts to speak
The earth starts to shudder.

The moon is like a policeman to me
Because I feel there are no robbers.
The night makes me feel as if I am his best friend.

His eyes are like big twinkles
And he wears a black suit.
He has long, dyed, blue hair.
His mouth is like a half-moon
He lives in the big place called:
The universe.

Michael Dodd (11)
The Richard Heathcote CP School

GLADIATOR

He enters the arena, as if he is king,
His sword held high, brightly shining,
He takes one step forward; and looks up into the light.
He thinks to himself will I win the fight?
The pain of the cut, the fear of the blood,
He tried to escape and he thought he could
One more last slash and he is no more
He never wanted to fight that cold war.
The crowd cheered loudly for the battle is done
And all for what, a few minutes fun?
The crowd erupt from the stand,
And the victor of the battle gets another gold band.

Ashleigh Bowers (11)
The Richard Heathcote CP School

A TREE'S LIFE

I am a tree;
I'm a hundred years old,
I'll tell you the story if you want to listen.
I was born as a seed in America,
A lady planted me in winter,
That night I slept so comfortably,
Snuggled up in my little seed,
So many days I slept in there,
That I got very bored.
One day in spring I was so big that the seed cracked,
How nice it was to feel the air,
Rush round me like some bees.
I stretched right out my one little branch,
And enjoyed the peaceful air.

Kevin Pepper (10)
The Richard Heathcote CP School

A CYCLE OF A TREE'S LIFE

When autumn was around I was a seed.
I was buried in soil and weed.
By a lady who liked to garden in every way.
She watered me twice a day.

In winter when I was just growing,
She put something in the ground for me to stop flopping.
I was surrounded by bigger trees
And a dark shade came upon me.

In spring I was taller but not as big as the others
I felt like I had more sisters and brothers.
I stood proud when the lady had visitors
My roots started to pop out of the ground.

In summer I was old and the other trees had gone
Then I started to get worried that I would go soon too.
One day I got dragged to a truck
But I hope other trees will have a better life than me.

Carl Madeley (10)
The Richard Heathcote CP School

TREES

I started as a lonely seed
I was planted in the soil
Where I grew to be a fine tree,
With my lovely family.
I make friends with the wind
Every day he whistles and howls at me
I wave my elegant branches back
Sometimes he blows my branches
Or sometimes he blows me about.
I grow bigger in the summer
Then lose my lovely leaves,
Which fall like snowflakes to the ground
During winter I feel old and miserable
But still I stand in the same old spot.

Kirstie Prince (11)
The Richard Heathcote CP School